Early Visual Skills

Written by Sue Lambert and Sandi Rickerby

Published by World Teachers Press®

Order Number 2-5102
ISBN 1-58324-024-1

A B C D E F 03 02 01 00 99

Educational Resources
395 Main Street
Rowley, MA 01969
www.worldteacherspress.com

Foreword

The *Early Skills Series* of books is designed to give students practice in a range of early reading, writing and number activities as well as to develop fine motor skills in the early years.

Early Skills Series – Early Visual Skills contains activities requiring students to find likenesses and differences among varied pictures and graphics. Students may be asked to match, order, draw, and/or color according to the instructions given.

The worksheets can be used to motivate students to work independently, increase their concentration span and develop their ability to work in an orderly fashion; encouraging them to take pride in the presentation of their work at the same time.

The worksheets are bold, uncluttered and visually appealing to young students. They contain instructions in graphic form, thereby requiring minimum support from you. They can be used to teach a new skill or reinforce and consolidate those already taught.

Other books in this series are: *Early Skills Series – Counting and Recognition to Five*
Early Skills Series – Addition to Five
Early Skills Series – Cutting Activities

Contents

Teacher Information

Introduction

Development of perceptual and fine motor skills in the early years is extremely important if students are to have a good grounding to progress to the next level of development. The *Early Skills Series* is designed to give practice in the aforementioned areas in a range of early reading, writing and number areas of the curriculum.

The worksheets are motivational and designed to encourage students to work independently wherever possible. This encourages high self-esteem, increases concentration span and develops the ability to work in a logical and orderly fashion.

The clear layout of each worksheet allows the student to concentrate solely on the task at hand. The large, open artwork appeals to students and has been drawn at the appropriate level for students' fine motor skill development.

Suggested Implementation

The *Early Skills Series* can be implemented easily into any existing program.

1. Familiarize students with the icons on pages 6 and 7. These pages can be enlarged, colored and displayed in a prominent position within the classroom. Students can then refer to the icons whenever they need to.

2. Develop recognition and understanding of the key words shown on the worksheets. Students may learn to read these words as sight words. Completing this will help develop their independence in completing the worksheet.

3. Discuss and explain each worksheet after all students have their worksheet in front of them.
    (a) Students sit on the mat area. You have an enlarged version of the worksheet.
    (b) Discuss the icons at the top of the page. Students can offer you the instructions for the page.
    (c) Work through the page, showing the students the completed product.
    (d) Students move back to their own work area to complete the worksheet independently.

4. Worksheets can be collected and viewed to determine areas of need for each student or the whole class group.

Teacher Information

Instructions

The instructions provided on each worksheet are in graphic form, thereby requiring minimal support from you. A key, explaining each graphic, is located on pages 6 and 7.

Benefits

The benefits of the *Early Skills Series* are many.

1. You can readily evaluate where each student is having success or difficulty.
2. Students are provided with the opportunity to work independently.
3. Students develop perceptual and fine motor skills in the areas of early reading, writing and numbers.
4. Students become familiar with a general range of instructional text.
5. Students are able to develop logic and work in an orderly fashion.
6. The worksheets are highly motivational.
7. The program is easy to implement into any classroom.

Conclusion

The *Early Skills Series* provides worksheets to cover *Early Visual Skills, Cutting, Counting and Recognition to Five* and *Addition to Five*; significant areas for student development during the early years of education. A solid grounding in these areas ensures smooth progression onto the next level of development. The activities are designed to allow the students to experience success, developing confidence and a positive self-image toward themselves as a learner.

Key-Early Visual Skills

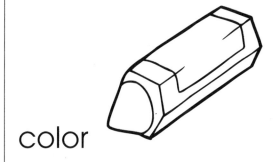

color

Color the pictures.

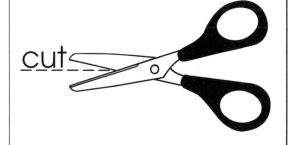

cut

Cut along the dotted lines.

glue

Glue into the correct place.

join

Draw a line to the matching picture.

1. group   2. color

1. color   2. cut ✂   3. glue

1. color

2. cut

3. glue

Name: _____ Date: _____

1. color 2. cut 3. glue

Early Skills Series – *Early Visual Skills*   World Teachers Press®

1. color

2. cut

3. glue

1. color

2. cut

3. order

4. glue

Early Skills Series – *Early Visual Skills*

1. color 2. _cut_ ✂ 3. o○◯ order 4. 🫙 glue

1. color   2. cut ✂   3. glue

Name: _____   Date: _____

1. color   2. _cut_ ✂   3. glue   4. ☐☐☐ order

glue

glue

glue

glue

glue

World Teachers Press®   Early Skills Series – *Early Visual Skills*   19

Name: _____ Date: _____

1. ✏️ join   2. ▭ color

Early Skills Series – *Early Visual Skills*   World Teachers Press®

Name: _____ Date: _____

1. color   2. cut ✂   3. glue

1 ... 9

9

1

World Teachers Press®   Early Skills Series – *Early Visual Skills*   29

1. color

2. cut

3. glue

1 9

9

1

 World Teachers Press®

Name: _____ Date: _____

1. draw **2.** color

1. draw 2. color

1. color **2.** _cut_ **3.** o order **4.** glue

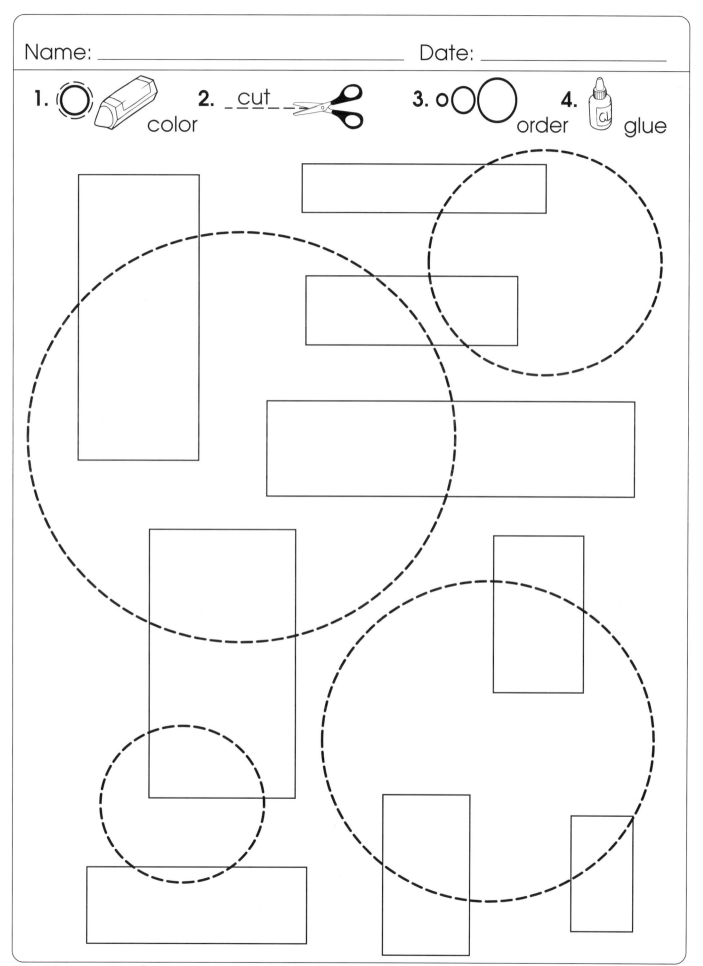

1. color 2. cut 3. order 4. glue

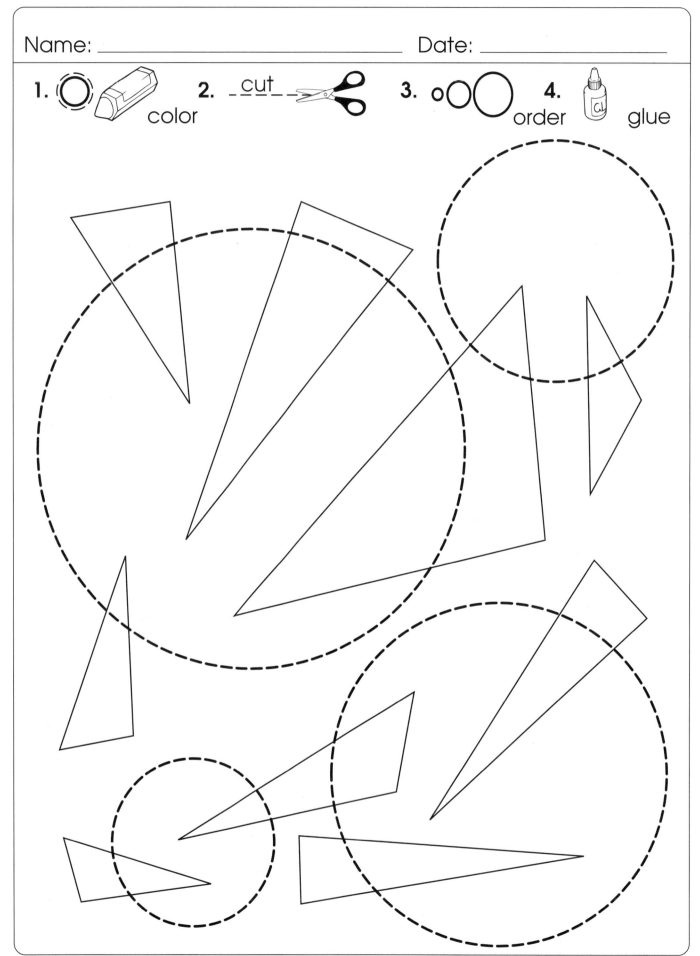

Name: _____ Date: _____

1. color   **2.** _cut_ ✂   **3.** glue

1. color   2. cut   3. order   4. glue

1. color   **2.** cut ✂   **3.** glue

1. color

2. cut

3. glue

Early Skills Series – *Early Visual Skills* World Teachers Press®

1. draw   **2.** color

Name: _____   Date: _____

1. draw   **2.** color

1. draw **2.** color

1. color ☆ – yellow ☁ – blue 🐟 – red 🍐 – green

Early Skills Series – *Early Visual Skills*
World Teachers Press®